Sleep on Needles

poems

Richard Lyons

Finishing Line Press
Georgetown, Kentucky

Sleep on Needles

Copyright © 2023 by Richard Lyons
ISBN 979-8-88838-179-3 First Edition
All rights reserved under International and Pan-American Copyright Conventions. No part of this book may be reproduced in any manner whatsoever without written permission from the publisher, except in the case of brief quotations embodied in critical articles and reviews.

ACKNOWLEDGMENTS

Thanks to my students and colleagues at Mississippi State University. Thanks to Dave Wojahn, Joe Powell, Mike Fredson, Bruce Cohen, Susan Prospere, Jeff Greene, Dave Theis, Stella Thorp, Gerry Thorp, Katherine Reynolds, Jody Stewart, Lisa Lewis, Gary Myers, Brad Vice, Katie Pierce, Mike Kardos, Becky Hagenston, Troy Derego, Patrick Creevy, Susie Creevy, Kelly Marsh, Sonny Ramaswamy, Gita Ramaswamy, Dinah Cox, and Ralph Burns for their support and their works.

Publisher: Leah Huete de Maines
Editor: Christen Kincaid
Cover Art: Gary Myers
Author Photo: Megan Bean / Mississippi State University
Cover Design: Elizabeth Maines McCleavy

Order online: www.finishinglinepress.com
also available on amazon.com

Author inquiries and mail orders:
Finishing Line Press
PO Box 1626
Georgetown, Kentucky 40324
USA

Table of Contents

Itinerant Prayer 1

Memory's Fog 2

Allium 3

Where I've Been, Where I'm Going 4

Ecology 5

To the Midnight Zone 6

Easter Sunday 7

Unstuck 8

Etiquette Chaffs My Psyche 9

The Sound of Chainsaws 10

Creatures from the Marsh 11

On the Margins of Development 12

The Pleasures of Moving Backwards 13

Everywhere Home 14

Sun 15

With Two Passages from Wallace Stevens 16

Homeopathy 17

A History of the Body 18

Komodo Dragon 19

Shadows Coming Apart 20

Flying 21

Thermogenic 22

Notes 23

for Leah Giniusz, Bill Olsen, and Nancy Eimers

Itinerant Prayer

I've read a late troubadour mourning the loss
of artisanal skills, our slums not lasting
as long as ancient temples.

Hanging like kittens from cats' mouths
is a posture our defenses won't permit.
St. John the Baptist survived the desert

to preach scant details of the Messiah.
Hannibal's army crossed the Alps
in the cold of winter. I descend a cave

to hear a bat colony nurse their pups
above a river of guano. Some people
can still carry water vessels on their heads

over rough terrain. Geologists argue,
distinguishing rain from wind erosion,
to construct alternative tales of the Sphinx.

A Florida condo leans on substandard rebar.
Feral cats hop broken shards after the collapse.
A boy summons cats with a saucer of milk.

He won't get scratched if he permits the cats
to determine their own order. Strays' hierarchy
or Robin Hood tales. Lord, let us sleep on needles.

Memory's Fog

Horned beetles bore holes in the cones.
The sequoia seeds ride chance.

A nautilus hums its own convolutions.
Gulls cry while they navigate winds,

a chorus inside memory's fog.
I wonder if bones are made of chalk,

a thousand sea creatures that forgot
they floated as autonomous creatures.

Allium

A long time ago, when I was ten,
my body shredded glory like coleslaw.

My St. Vitus nerves shook the roll
down to just hotdog and mustard.

On the Waterfront, Brando in the car
is bawling for us all. Sometimes

garlic flowers turn the color of a bruise
on an old man's arm. Sometimes

they sway in bluish shades depending
on how they'll swallow their insignificance.

Where I've Been, Where I'm Going

Shoulders swing a reaper's scythe
the way I assume a swath would cut

when a scythe sweeps. Grasshoppers
fly from thick grass to find clefts

we'll never guess. One affronted one
sputters after it hits my chest

and drops, stunned and alive.
It persists, or should I say reverie

persists while fog seeps the ease
of a few trees. Waves of misery

spare me, cresting outside thought.
I wipe my hairline with a sleeve

and sip water. A glacier plummets.
A million grasses sprout from river silt.

Ecology

A man covers a canvas
with the oil from an oil spill.

It will slip down the canvas
via its own physics. Give it time.

Disarmed human, de-boned fish,
eggshell color remastering itself.

To the Midnight Zone

Memory sluices my blood to zinc and salt,
spreading individuality into waves of sand
the crabs will smooth to blinking apertures.
Even if I feel the nicks on the door jamb
that mother would cut to track my height
with a yellow no. 2 pencil, the specific
layers of my body surrender one by one.

Each house key drops to homely pearl,
and rats climb each other's back.
A bottlenose dolphin drags what it eats
beneath the buoyancy a swim bladder lifts.
Everything hides, claims Heraclitus.
The midnight zone spawns strange shapes
that defy the hysterics loneliness mourns
out to the edges we can't calibrate.
Cold shoals massage fear to bioluminescence.

Easter Sunday

One Easter Sunday, I ruined crepes with my inattention.
They tasted like what I imagine
burnt Elmer's Glue would.

Memory decants identity when our backs are turned.
Blue whales sing high-pitched songs.
Between the blades of kelp forest,

fish spin their fins. Ancestral skin thickens to numb fur.

Unstuck

Giant mouths sift krill. Look, Mom,
no hands, squeaks a spotted Greenland shark.

I come unstuck.
Good thing attachments are so resilient.

A match box sits beside a mortuary urn.
An adding machine tape

curls over the table like a spider-monkey's tail.
Terror is behind the phenomenon of breathing.

Etiquette Chaffs My Psyche

Strata (plural) challenge the shorthand,
but logic flatters a house with environs.
The early Christians may've built churches
over the top of toppled Druid temples

because two heads aren't better than one.
What becomes of a dead man's house?
The banana you found on his counter
was almost ripe. An old galaxy explodes

with methane and dust eating the oxygen—
a green vapor glowing on computer model.
But my imagined perspective is a sailboat
as it tacks into the wind. First it turns west

and then it turns east as if each port of call
is too whimsical a topic to utter in the voice
of the holy books. Now they say the Floating
Gardens of Babylon are located outside Nineveh,

aka the town of Mosul—zealots chop heads off.
Conduits trickling water is the voice of Allah,
but soothing sand riding the wind may obscure it
as ancients use a shaduf to raise water to the parapets.

The Sound of Chainsaws

There are no hours in this day of which
I am speaking. There is little personality
in the voice whose sound is rising, waiting

for a reply. Estuaries offer so much protein
that anthropologists assume a migratory route
followed the coast 400 feet beneath the waves.

Deficient bones of an ancient girl signal
alternative migratory routes from Alaska
to the Yucatan caves flooded in our instant,

a labyrinth mimicking our skulls' conduits.
My clavicle and scapula undulate involuntarily
every time I hear a chainsaw decimate trees.

I'm convinced I'm brachiating with gibbons
when I smell the stunned scent of cut wood.
Chaos may be a regular joe with no education

or grace, but he may caress the way a bee's fur
alights on pistils. Can't I tune out the buzzsaw?
I am weighing a letter so lithe I want to affix

to it a foreign stamp depicting the Tower of Pisa
so that the letter arrives in a dead letter office
in America and every inch of protocol can insist

it be followed to the letter. Here I'm acting coy
to pretend I don't yearn for some oblique signal
heading back to my senses each time I whisper

into God's curly hair. Li Po just cast his poems
on the River of Heaven. I want to love everyone
while I whisper, and a wail turns a screw in my skull.

Creatures from the Marsh

> *There was love in us, things we spoke to each other*
> *in the evening or on deathbeds, the eyes frank at last.*
> —Loren Eiseley

Aches decay like eggplant beneath leaves.
Restraint is in short supply

as far as physiology flows.
Epithelial cells scatter to the horizons

as the universe expands, keeping time
with the lassoes of tendrils.

There's still time, but our energies surge
and then subside like the cicadas' cries

while the cities entangle words in orbits
around someone's favorite keystone.

We begin with love, but chaos overwhelms
with love's multiplication. I thrash my cowlick.

I lick my paws. I eat berries, peat, greens—one
rabid cannibal slipping as wraith through palimpsest.

On the Margins of Development

Rats and birds pretty much leave each other alone.
A beaver dam pools twenty little ponds.

If this marsh is seething, the hours can't ratchet it.
Cats adapt to every climate, the jaguar's strong jaw

breaking caiman or capybara. Water doesn't hate
didactic beasts the way I crave elemental mystery.

Everything craved recedes, everything receding
is sought. I cross in a boat and then a pair of boots.

Forms of energy survive our limited detection.
Amid these grass islands, mosquitoes pick me apart.

The Pleasure of Moving Backwards

The almond trees are always thirsty, the white
almost swirl of Virgin's bower's silky fruit.
The earth creates ethereal vistas to approach.

Seeing things up close isn't disappointing.
Pour the sea into my tea. Take it or leave it?
Isn't that how we drink the diluted elixirs?

When I'm happy, I'm not thinking. I pout
from time to time. Reverie insists on its own
concept of time taking me out to its edges,

sun and water in short supply. I will imagine
a sympathetic friend snipping a weed flower
or sitting to watch a doe browsing new leaves.

The surf inside the skull—nautilus convolutions—
allows our dim eardrums to trigger a synapse.
A million grasses blow all at once to variables

caressing the cheek, the chin. My radical choices
hurt too many people. If a burrow has built-in exits,
I may just last forever. Breathing starts and finishes,

the lake shushing ashore, a crayfish flashing a claw.
All bets are off, every either-or. I envy an otter
as it swims under water. I envy a marsh hawk

piercing my soul's toothpick. Hummingbirds
turning nectar to wingbeats cross miles of ocean.
The questing spores float and dissipate like smoke.

What we see isn't liquid but the glint spending every bit
of loose change stacked on bedside dresser. Martens
nibble our electrons. Thrift dies as we thrive w/o names.

Everywhere Home

A nest comes drifting down to earth. The river
makes a sound keen to deer, vireo, and rat.
The moon is an animal drinking on the wing
as far as salt estuaries, castaway's island, kelp raft.

The moon licks the salt on bark or rock, the taste
of blood turning sweet, the indigence of moths,
and the separate parts agility hums inside the flute
of my femur till everywhere swears it's home.

Living requires we acknowledge each suffering
but then forget each as fast as we can,
the crows mobbing a hawk that swoops close
to the little corvids. The earth is concentrating

before it disperses. I remain separate to belong
to what is outside my skull. The panther has a twenty
square-mile territory though the measures seem paltry,
the way a murmuration soothes sunflowers' nodding heads.

Sun

There's no time left. I am waiting.
A peach ripens, hanging in the sun.

I imagine the tip of my tongue
feeling peach fuzz. The nape

of someone I can't remember,
my hand brushing the hair aside to kiss.

With Two Passages from Wallace Stevens

I've forgotten where my underground caches
lie hidden. *It is the human that is alien,*
The human that has no cousin in the moon.

And to feel that the light is rabbit-light,
In which everything is meant for you
And nothing need be explained.

Never mind the burrows and escarpments.
There is so much to be remembered
I am bound to let something slip my brain.

To say someone has his feet planted firmly
on this earth may be less of a compliment
than it was in years past—ancient or more recent.

Don't we all confuse memories with dreams?
I crawl through what branches out beneath my feet.
Mutual agreements between rootlets and fungi, muskrat and fox.

Homeopathy

A bishop flicks a holy water stick,
and the sting catches my left eye.

I go down on all fours like a piece
of driftwood. Crabs move like yoyos.

A tincture of iodine with quinine
may help heal everything. My heart

speeds up and decelerates all at once.
From my femur, I lick a few droplets.

I feel lightheaded amid wild carrot,
Queen Ann's lace, bird's nest. By any

of its names, it's so edible. Swallowtail
butterflies shiver their finery. A bicycle

finds itself entangled in vines. A great
blue heron high-steps it, a major domo

or marionette. The tops of my feet turn
reddish-brown. I'm receding from myself.

Calculations trivialize themselves. Tropical
depressions swell my solar plexus till it winces.

A History of the Body

Did I lick empty the termite Colossus?
Did I dry every plate? Do earthquakes

eventually shimmy to confetti or dandruff?
The body is permeable, like limestone or sand.

We transplant the Hanging Gardens
of Babylon to a more secret site. It's a question

of moisture and arable soil. My eyes are dry,
and I'm blinking like a lighthouse.

We pile knowledge on top of knowledge,
and the cairn topples. We itch with a rash of questions,

starting with cradle cap. We touch scars. Understanding
insufficient, we must remember every moment of our lives.

Komodo Dragon

I remember a game of bocce on flat sand.
An old man removed his leather belt
to measure whether his ball or his opponent's
were closer to the pallino.

I should probably pretend vocalizations
won't save me. My tongue tastes the sea air.
My ears are little circles. I puff air
through my nostrils, and bob my skull.

I'm pretty sure I won't be acceptable.
Ambition is unattractive, susceptible.
I've carried Christ on my shoulder as Christopher
once did. Wounds wail like a chorus of disciples.

Shadows Coming Apart

> *for nothing is so brutally savage than the man*
> *who is not aware he is a shadow.*
> —Loren Eiseley

Tributaries flow, as well as weeping tendrils,
photosynthetic horns and horns
made of keratin, just like our fingernails,

someone adds each time in afterthought,
as if the human were the hub of breathing.
Everyone disappears, two friends from ALS.

One from cancer, one an enlarged heart.
Two wolves gnaw the carcass of a juvenile
moose that the flying insects drove crazy,

swarming everywhere, weakening her past
saving. I'm walking with the husky Misu,
my friend Sonny's Eskimo dog descendant.

I sit on the ground, and a seep soaks the seat
of my pants. We're always out in the elements,
nest, burrow, escarpment. No matter how quietly

I walk, the birds go silent. What makes us think
we're anything more than a hiatus that has every right
to survive, the way a cat pauses in mid-step

if shadows move in relation to others coming apart,
each step or pause a humbling we may take to heart
or at least touch like alienation, words conjuring shadows.

Flying

Possibilities offer themselves to any boundary.
Hawks cross the sun. Owls haunt the moon.
Staying alive requires inattention.

I'm no better than either bird.
We learn the way words breathe
and fall, craved or unwanted. Some bouncer

stamped the back of my hand with a blacklight ship.
It took a week to wash off. Weissbier
might have gone right to my head

as years passed before I could form a question
in badly accented German. Maybe we accumulate lostness
the way we pack memories, flying faster than the speed of light.

Thermogenic

We hope language will lift the shadows
as easy as cedar waxwings relay a berry
down a line of birds even if the anchor
ends up choking on a breath of sedge.

An egg tooth cuts a marsh hawk's egg.
The parent-hawks eat the chicks' feces
or discard the stink across the forest
to keep hungry weasels at a distance.

An owl calls and then ceases calling.
My eyes run out to the edge of sound.
Off a trail, a monk's hood melts the ice
to climb from the dirt. The early bees

will sip the sinuses of this second cousin
of the jack-in-the-pulpit. If we tremble
w/o moving a muscle, maybe the mind
craves heat and chalks new cosmologies.

Notes:

The poem "Shadows Coming Apart" is in memory of the poets Judy Kleck Powell, John Kay, Lynda Schraufnagel, and Marty Scott.

Originally from Boston, **Richard Lyons** is the author of *Heart House* (Emrys Press, 2019), *Un Poco Loco* (Iris Books, 2016), *Fleur Carnivore*, winner of 2005 Washington Prize (Word Works, 2006), *Hours of the Cardinal* (University of South Carolina Press, 2000) and *These Modern Nights* (University of Missouri, 1988). He has been a recipient of a Nation "Discovery" Award and is Emeritus Professor of English and Creative Writing at Mississippi State University. He lives outside of Memphis with his wife.

www.ingramcontent.com/pod-product-compliance
Lightning Source LLC
Chambersburg PA
CBHW022128090426
42743CB00008B/1053